The Second Mile

HARRY EMERSON FOSDICK

Whosoever shall compel thee to
go one mile, go with him two

GROSSET & DUNLAP
Publishers :: New York
By arrangement with Association Press

The Second Mile

WHEN Iago says about Desdemona that "she holds it a vice in her goodness not to do more than is requested," he lays his discriminating finger on a trait of character not ordinarily worked up in the systems of ethics. Nowhere does he better justify his own comment on himself, "I am nothing if not critical." And it is precisely this trait of character on which Iago with his devilish ingenuity lighted for his evil purpose, that Jesus made the crown of the moral life. The distinctively Christian quality is to hold it a vice in our goodness not to do more than is requested.

Indeed, when it comes down to doing the bare stint of requirement, and nothing more, Jesus calls that "unprofitable." When he describes the servants who, after their day's work in the field, wait upon their lord at supper, he takes obvious satisfaction in the paradox that, though they have fulfilled their obligations from plowing in the morning to serving at night, they deserve no thanks at all. Lest his disciples should doubt the application, he says distinctly and peremptorily, "Even so ye also, when ye shall have done all the things that are commanded you, say, 'We are unprofitable servants; we have done that which it was our duty to do.'" Not until a man's willingness overflows his obligation, so that what he has to do is seen as a segment in the circle of what he would be willing to do, does he become what Jesus would call profitable—nor even what Shakespeare would count worthy a character like Desdemona.

Now, when the Sermon on the Mount faces us with those strict and startling injunctions to give coat and

cloak when a coat is wanted, or to
take two blows when one is offered,
or to travel two miles when but one
is compulsory—injunctions that are
either stark nonsense or supernally
divine sense—we are manifestly deal-
ing with a dramatic presentation of
this favorite and characteristic truth
of Jesus, that only an unstinted willingness to do more than anyone can
ask makes possible a liberal and Christian character.

To be sure, he stated his truth in an
austere and formidable way. His figures of speech startle us with their
severe requirements, and to those who
first heard them they must have been
bewildering in their difficulty. When
Jesus said, "Whosoever shall compel
thee to go one mile, go with him
two," a concrete picture rose before
his Jewish audience, a hateful picture
of a Roman soldier, under the sanc-
tion of his military law, compelling
a Jew to the defiling business of carry-
ing his burden for a mile. To hear
this new Rabbi say that under such

compulsion a Jew should be willing to go two must have clashed with the Jewish temper, as it would with the American. This sounded like gratuitous surrender of a man's just rights. This looked like generosity gone to seed. And any hearer, knowing the history of that Roman word "angario," whose Aramaic equivalent Jesus doubtless used when he said "compel," must have found acquiescence in Jesus' command even more unreasonable. As though it were the badge of tyranny, that word had been handed down by the Persian Empire to the Greek, and by the Greek to the Roman, and from the beginning it had stood for military power to impress into unwilling service all men or horses whose help the soldiery desired. The word was saturated with the hatefulness of age-long tyranny. The unrelenting visages of Persian satraps, Greek governors, and Roman generals were conjured up by its ominous sound, and Jesus' injunction to superabundant willingness was made by its use to seem impossibly difficult.

Nevertheless, the aptitude of the principle to our experience is obvious at least in this regard, that while the old military empires long since have gone and Roman soldiers no longer draft into grudging service, compulsion, as a permanent factor in human life, remains. Whether we face it Jesus' way or not, we must face it somehow. We do have our Roman couriers that light upon us trudging our chosen path and, whether we will or no, take us along with them. The word "must" belongs in our lives as truly as in any Jew's forced into service by an imperial messenger.

Young folk, like rollicking colts in a lush meadow, have preëminently the sense of freedom, but no colt ever pranced far without coming to a fence. One of the signs of dawning maturity appears when this first consciousness of liberty gives place to perception of limitations, to insight into the compelling power of necessity.

to audience that often hears the magisterial words "You must!" The body says "Must"; the demands of social life say "Must"; the necessities of business say "Must"; at every other milestone we meet a courier to impress us into service. Like springs, bubbling up in a first ecstasy of unfettered freedom, but soon finding that every brook has its banks, so men out of the youthful sense of unrestricted liberty flow into a life-course, held in on either side by unescapable necessities. Sooner or later every man finds his boundaries, and while poets may sing their songs of pathos over the fact, practical people have a more serious problem: to find out, that is, how a man ought to face life's compulsions, in what attitude of mind and spirit he should meet the "Must" of the world. And Jesus said, "Whosoever shall compel thee to go one mile, go with him two." At first sight that is about the strangest prescription for the trouble a man could well imagine. It proceeds upon the homœopathic principle that "like things cure like," and would drive out the poison of a disease by injecting more of the same kind. If you are compelled to go one mile, of your own free will go two, it says, and so defeat the malice of the necessity by voluntarily going it one better.

Indeed, it is clear that if the earth should say to two plants in a garden, "You must grow," and if one plant should accept the bare necessity, and sullenly grow its stint and no more, that would be slavish business with no glory in it. But if its companion should say: "It is my delight to grow! Come on, O Earth, with all your bounty! You say I must grow, but lo! I am twice as willing as you are to make me!" that would be a free plant, with worth and distinction in its growing. It is found true at even a cursory glance that the sting of compulsion is gone when a man is twice as willing to act as necessity is to make him.

The Second Mile

Now among all the ways in which we feel the Roman hand upon our shoulder, none is more unescapable than the compulsion of time. This is the most inevitable of all inevitable things. Tie what you will to the tail of the seconds, they are sublimely indifferent to your hindrances. If you watch the passing days closely, you find a tyrannic oppression in their noiseless and unceasing march. The Valley of Ajalon where the sun stands still and the retreating shadow on Ahaz's dial have long vanished into the limbo of the eternally lost. When in Congress the sergeant moves back the hands of the government clock, making an artifice of time to pass the last bills in, he must do it with a sardonic grin, for he knows what a futile fraud he is perpetrating on the sun, and how the constellations laugh at him. This slow inevitableness of time is a small matter indeed to the youth, but it puts compulsion on a man not easy to be glad about. So Jesus said to Peter, " When thou wast young thou girdedst thyself and wentest whither thou wouldst, but when thou shalt be old another shall gird thee and carry thee where thou wouldst not."

How men rebel against this un-evadable fatality! How they fret over declining powers, and grudgingly submit to limitation, like free lakes poured into narrowing canyons and tumbling upon themselves in fury! Because men take it so, because they enter their cramped confines with such ill grace, they make sorry business out of age, with never a touch of Rabbi Ben Ezra's mellow and radiant spirit:

" Grow old along with me,
The best is yet to be;
The last of life for which the first
was made!"

Rabbi Ben Ezra had the spirit of the second mile. His years were no less implacable in their compulsion and his limitations no less carking than is

the lot of other men, but he could see
in both years and limitations

" Machinery just meant
    To give thy soul its bent;
    Try thee and turn thee forth
    Sufficiently impressed."

And whenever you seek the secret of
this kind of age, you will not fail to
find a man who has gone the second
mile; who has faced time and said,
" O Time, you are a stern fellow,
but you have a godlike power of
beauty in you. You can make souls
deep and rich and fruitful, as you
make old violins musical with the
stored-up melodies of years; as you
make old wine perfect with the ripe-
ness of long generations. You say
that I 'must' go this mile with you,
but I am wise enough to look upon
my necessities as though they were
my luxuries, and I will go with you so
willingly that men shall learn from
me to say anew, ' The hoary head is a
crown of glory!'" The more one

The Elemental Must

considers it, the more it is clear that when a man must go one mile, the only spirit that can save his soul from bitterness is the willingness to go two.

There is another Roman also, who levies his draft upon us, and that is the Roman of work. Underneath every other practical necessity, is this elemental "must" of the breadwinner; and unless a man has been so hapless as to receive a legacy, youth's heaviest handicap, he needs no one to tell him what an inexorable master this necessity is. Now this compulsion, which sooner or later most men are sure to encounter, may be faced in one of two ways. If he will, a man may accept it doggedly and go about the demanded labor like the Sultan's Janizaries under the lash. He may take work as an unfortunately necessary part of life, and let himself be beaten to it by the cat-o'-nine-tails in the hand of Need. He may skimpingly perform the bare requirements and, hating his taskmaster as a ran-

corous old Jew hated a Roman courier, may bitterly trudge that one scant
mile, as unwilling as Bryant's "quar-
ry-slave at night scourged to his dun-
geon." That is one way to face the
necessity of work and thousands of
men with their eyes on the clock are
working that way to-day. Or if he
will, a man may rise to the measure
of Antonio Stradivari, in George El-
iot's poem, and say of his humblest
daily tasks what Stradivari said about
his violins:

"If my hand slacked
I should rob God, since he is fullest
   good,
Leaving a blank instead of violins.
* * * * *
                He could not make
Antonio Stradivari's violins
Without Antonio."

Whenever a man glorifies his work
in that way he has gone the second
mile; he has translated duty into
privilege. He has seen that while
God supplies quarries he never carves

My Work My Friend

statues or piles cathedrals save by the
hand of a man; he has perceived that
the earth was not built like Aladdin's
Palace, by magic spells for lazy oc-
cupancy, but is an unfinished world
into which men are ushered in time
to bear a part in its completion; and
he has reached the dignity of believ-
ing that every honest piece of work
is coöperation with God in building
the universe. Such a man can follow the Master's word and can give
glad welcome to the necessity of
work, as it accosts him on the road.
He can say, and mean it too, "O
Work, you are my best friend in dis-
guise. God sent you to me. You come
with a stern face, but your heart is
full of strength and courage and good
cheer. You demand that I travel with
you that one hard mile? Then, my
task, doff that scowl, for to the limit
of my strength I am twice as willing
to work as you are to make me."
Work, greeted like that, loses the
frown of compulsion and begins to
smile. When a man works that way

13

because he thinks it is his Father's business, feels that it is his meat and drink to do the will of him that sent him, wishes there were more hours in the day than twenty-four, and dreams of Heaven as a place where a man can work all the time at his best and never be tired—all the slavery of work has vanished for such a man and he and his task, good friends, walk arm in arm, and will be sorry when the second mile is done. It looks as though Jesus were right, after all. The way to avoid the slavishness of necessity is of your own accord to be willing, if possible, to do more than is demanded. The first mile alone is drudgery. The glory comes with the second mile!

Another kind of compulsion faces every man in some degree—the compulsion of limiting circumstances and restricted powers that shut him up to narrow and obscure activities. There are more people than perhaps we think, whose aspirations for preëminence have been snuffed to a smoulder. Some aspired to be musicians, some authors, others teachers, preachers, missionaries; they had perhaps to start with talents equal to their dreams; but the thwarting circumstance, the broken health gradually closed them in and shortly they found themselves hedged around, with a stern Roman peremptorily saying, "You must live your lives here!" We all face this one way or another. If not the external circumstance, it is that unescapable limitation of our own individuality, the most vexatious handicap of all. For a man to accept himself and start with only one talent, if God has not given him ten, is difficult business. "Das verdammte Ich," cried Goethe, and we all know what he meant.

Some one has compared man to an actor able to play many rôles but restricted to one; and any virile man, facing the fascinating opportunities of the world's work and feeling the latent possibility of many accomplishments and ministries, knows that the necessity of choosing one rôle, or having it thrust upon him, of playing that and not another, is no less tyrannic than a Roman courier to a Jew. Other compulsions may be more grievous to a feeble man, but to the nobler character it is the limitation of life's possible investment that presses hardest. He wants the whole farm and is confident that he could farm it, but lo! this small garden plot with a hedge all around.

Now one solution of the problem is both popular and easy. He may raise his little crop of vegetables in that narrow garden plot and sit down in bitterness behind his hedge to eat them. He may look over his meager boundaries at the bigger farms of stronger men and envy their more extensive operations. He may take his spite out by a cynical disparagement of the whole business of living anyhow, or he may wax melodramatic with Henley and talk about his head being "bloody but unbowed." He may even assume the Titanic pose and

The Titanic Pose

grandiloquently dare high heaven, de-
claiming like Thompson in his "City
of Dreadful Night,"

"I vow
That not for all Thy power, furled or
　unfurled,
For all the temples to Thy glory built,
Would I assume the ignominious
　guilt
Of having made such men in such a
　world!"

In a word, he may incarnate the one-
mile spirit and grow surly, rebellious
and morose within his narrow hedges.
　If, however, that does not seem a
knightly attitude, there appears no
alternative short of Jesus' way, who
evidently would have us say about
this same meager plot, "Well, it is
not much to start with, but, O Roman
of Necessity, you need not think that
I am going to do only what you command, merely live here and raise
enough to eat. I am going to make
this little place so beautiful that pas-

sers-by will stop to enjoy it. It is not large, but fair flowers grow in small places. You require me to live here, but I will go twice as far as that. I will not only live here, but I will make it worth while living here; and these very hedges which you say must always bind me in, I will husband until they are as fragrant as English hawthorne or Scotch heather, and people who cried, 'What cruel limitations!' shall yet say, 'What a beautiful hedge!'"

History loves to record the names of men who conquered the malice of their fate by this spirit of the second mile—men like the old Greek chosen in a joke to be town scavenger, who filled the office with such high serviceableness that thereafter in all Greece the office was an honor; men like blind Huber becoming the great scientist, or blind Fawcett becoming Postmaster-General of England; men like Cervantes using an imprisonment to begin "Don Quixote," or Bunyan glorifying Bedford Jail with the "Pil-

grim's Progress"; men of the spirit
of those four marines from the Brit-
ish ship " Wager " of whom Steven-
son tells us, who, compelled to remain
on a desert island because the lifeboat
could hold no more, stood on the shore
and gave three cheers when the boat
pulled off—with a " God save the
King! " for a tiger. These men history delights to honor, for, in the end,
time endorses God's evaluations. And
where in humbler expressions this
same spirit of the second mile is
found, as when the young woman
wrote her friend out of her invalid-
ism, " At first I thought somehow to
make the best of it, but now I am
planning how to make the most of it,"
every man with a heart for chivalry
pays homage. These folk of the more
abundant willingness travel with us
the first hard mile of compulsion, but
they make it beautiful with the second mile of consecration. That bare
compulsion, taken alone, is grim, but
when we rise to say " I will make
my narrow boundaries a garden of

the Lord where he may walk as he did in Eden in the cool of the day," the cruel necessity glows with a divine meaning, and a glory appears in the limited life—the glory of the second mile.

When we carry this principle out from the realm of such inevitable necessities as time and work and personal limitation, into the sphere of moral obligation, its applicability becomes all the more clear. Some things are sternly demanded of men by the regulations of the social life. The formal obligations of the marriage covenant, for example, can be enforced. There is an irreducible minimum of duty which Public Opinion insists on expecting from wives and husbands, parents and children. Like some old Roman, the Social Conscience, sometimes speaking with the voice of legal enactment, comes to every one of us, and says of the absolutely necessary duties of family relationship, "You must do these things."

There are households, moreover,

The One-mile Home

where this minimum marks the outer boundary within which the whole life of the family moves. They do just as much as they have to do and no more. The household is run in the spirit with which a miser pays taxes. Any overflow of spontaneous love, any voluntering of surplus kindliness is unknown. They keep the prohibitions of the law, and look for a home to come of it, like Gasparoni, the Italian bandit who hoped for heaven because he had never committed murder on Friday. They are one-mile folk and they make a one-mile home.

But it is the unnecessary courtesies, the unexpected presents brought from the city, the uncalled-for thoughtfulness of lovers, the surprises of kindliness over and above what can be required—this superabundance makes a real home. Here the difference lies between a parent and a father; between progeny and sons; between a housewife and a mother. Let a housewife be never so faithful about her tasks, determined to do them well,

21

with resolution keeping the home neat, the children well provided; yet any man who has had a real mother knows at once that such description leaves the glory out. The real mother did her duties too, but there was something more—a radiance that glowed through her simple tasks like a quiet dawn in summer, an ampleness of love as though she moved in realms where rules had been forgotten, that made her human affection liberal like the love of the Eternal God. Her ministries could not be so commonplace as to let you utterly escape the secret influence of the fact that with unsearchable desire she had prayed for you first. Her spirit was greater than her deeds and suffused them; and as you remember her now, you think not so much of her particular ministries as of that unwearied willingness to overpass all boundaries in loving you. The last thing you can ever forget is that luminous tenderness which, like God's sunshine on the just and the unjust, sought you out in whatsoever merit or demerit you might be, to find you as Christ found the world, not that he might condemn it, but that the world through him might be saved. All true mothers live in the spirit of the second mile.

Like the Word of God brooding over chaos and making a world of it, this surplus tenderness creates homes out of households. There are few things more pathetic than a one-mile family, but the crown of all human relationships and the hope of the country is the two-mile home, where always "the cup runneth over."

What this principle of Jesus does, then, when applied to our moral life, is clear. It divides a man's conduct into two parts, the compulsory and the voluntary, the things he must do and the things he chooses to do, the first mile and the second. It says, moreover, that only as the voluntary overspreads and saturates the necessary can life cease to be slavery and come to its full meaning of dignity and value. There is an essential nobility that belongs only to the soul who can say with Jesus, "No man taketh my life from me. I lay it down of myself." Until willingness overflows obligation, men fight as conscripts instead of following the flag as patriots.

Now, with reference to this spirit of the second mile, men are divided into well-defined classes, of which the lowest are clearly those miserable folk who like Shylock are forever after their rights. Their attitude toward men is that of a collector seeking payment on protested bills. They are specialists in the exaction of what is due them. They interpret duty as a customs officer does—to mean not what he owes men, but what men owe him. Such men reveal themselves by their instinctive attitude toward clearly stated moral obligations, such as, "Thou shalt not bear false witness against thy neighbor." Facing this command, some will cry, desiring all their rights, "Is my neighbor, then, bearing false witness against me?" and some will

24

Privilege First

search their souls with the question of duty, "Am I bearing false witness against my neighbor?" Rights or duties, you can interpret any commandment either way, and it is the relative emphasis a man places here that measures the first stage in his character building. Not till duty looms larger than rights is a man truly moral. But neither the one nor the other is the test of Christian character. Christianity begins when the sense of privilege in service becomes greater than both rights and duties. For us to be Christian is to be more willing to serve a man than he is to demand it; to go the second mile; to forgive seventy times seven; to pray on our Calvaries for the men who put us there; to act, that is, as no one has the right to require of us, and to feel about it all that our meat and drink are to do the will of him that sent us. The essential word of Christianity is love and that means superabundant willingness to help. A man becomes really Christian when the sense of joy in ministry overflows both rights and duties and submerges them.

And just here is the real worth of the moral life. So long as Wordsworth sings Duty, "Stern Daughter of the Voice of God," he is but on the threshold of the matter. It is only when he rises in his climax to say:

"Yet thou dost wear
The Godhead's most benignant grace;
Nor know we anything so fair
As is the smile upon thy face:
Flowers laugh before thee on their
 beds
And fragrance in thy footing treads,"

only then has he come to the heart of it. Duty is never worthily done until it is performed by a man who loves it so that he would gladly do more if he could. Some men say of their duties, "I must"; some men say, "I ought"; some men say, "I want to, let me at it." These are the three tones of life. One man is the slave of his necessities; one, the grim moralist doing his duty; one, the man of an abounding sense of privilege in life, who feels all blessings large with God's favor, all trials meaningful with purpose, all duty a glorious prerogative. Though the gross output of moral living may seem in each case to be the same, these lives are not of one spiritual family. A duty done grudgingly and the same duty done willingly are after all not the same. All sense of compulsion and of obligation is only underground foundation for the real temple, whose altar-song is forever, "I delight in the law of the Lord."

As the real worth of the moral life lies in this attitude of more abundant willingness, so the whole joy of the moral life lies there too. It is because of their unwillingness to go the second mile that men make such desperate labor out of going the first. When Paul finds himself with his hard road to travel—an arduous journey all the way from the midnight escape at Damascus to the headsman's axe at Rome

—he does not, like the lesser souls, spoil it by desiring to go half instead. "I must" is alien from his spirit; "I ought," an occasional but not dominant tone; "Thanks be to God who counted me worthy, appointing me to be his minister," that is Paul's overflowing zeal which took the sting from the first mile's obligation. If a friend ask a favor, saying, "I have a right to demand that as a friend," and you reply, "Man, stop talking about rights. I am more willing to make that sacrifice than you are to ask me," by that you have transformed obligation from drudgery to privilege. So Paul wrote to Philemon, making request of service from him, and said, "Without thy mind I would do nothing, that thy goodness should not be as of necessity, but of free will"; and thereby he suggested the only way to find joy in duty. The penurious moralist stingily expending himself no farther than the law requires, is a pitifully sad fellow, who has never learned that it is hard work serving as a drafted man in a battle you would like to avoid, but that it is glorious business fighting as a volunteer for a cause you love.

There are a thousand little ways in which we can put this to the test: If we have money and are pestered by requests for its expenditure, what a cure for impatience to recognize that it is more to our interest to have our stewardship rightly accomplished than it can be to any other man's, so that even if we cannot give to a particular cause we can send the petitioner away with the feeling that we were more willing to give than he was to ask us! If we have talents and are worn threadbare by the continual demands upon us, what a cure for the requirement's malice to know that it is more to our interest to do all the good we can than it can be to any other man's —and so to meet each request with a willingness to do even more if we are able. Any child knows the magic of this divine remedy if he has ever dragged his reluctant feet toward the

berry patch under orders to pick two
quarts, and then has solved the problem of his uncomfortable duty by cry-
ing, "What fun! I'll surprise the
family by picking four!" Drudgery
is all redeemed by that.

When a man, however, attempts
this attitude toward all the duties of
his life, tries to make it the solvent
for his moral drudgeries, he finds that
reasonably to be more than willing to
do all he ought to do, so that his volunteering outruns the demands of men
upon him, implies a view of life that
taxes the limit of his faith. A man
can say, "I must" in atheism; he can
say, "I ought" in bare morality; but
to say "I want to" as though there
were a great privilege in living, as
though it "means intensely and means
good," as though purpose were there
because the world had been thought
through and willed through and loved
through by a Father, as though des-
tinies were ahead in which the mean-
ings of all sacrifice would come to
their apocalypse in glory "exceeding

abundant above all we can ask or think "—that means a religious view of the world. Only when a man believes that there is a Person to receive our consecration, whose service is perfect freedom, and whose love constraineth to that noblest motive for all duty doing, the gratitude of love to One who loved us first; only then can he reasonably feel the more abundant willingness in sacrificial service. If there is some one able to "keep that which we commit unto him," so that nothing is ever wasted, no serviceable deed, no love, no aspiration, but

"All we have willed or hoped or
    dreamed of good shall exist,
  Not its semblance, but itself,"

then we can say, "I want to." Only the man of Christian faith, who sees the Eternal God mirrored in the character and purposes of Christ can reasonably accept the privilege of Christian service. A man can stumble the first mile almost anyhow, but no man can travel the second mile without God!

Indeed here we enter the very Holy of Holies of religious living. As the spirit of the second mile so inevitably demands the Christian God to make it reasonable, so the same spirit is the best interpreter of the life which such a God inspires. To many people religious living is an affair of negative prohibitions, and they walk in the presence of God like an embarrassed courtier at the salon of Louis XIV, conscious chiefly of what they must not do. Their righteousness is exhausted in what they refrain from. "They are just as good as trying not to be bad can make them." Or if a man has graduated from this idea of God as a Sinaitic Lawgiver, who spends his odd moments checking up the accounts of folk who have transgressed his prohibitions, he may still conceive religious living as a matter of positive rules and regulations, ceremonial and moral, whose observance is the whole of duty. This man is the kind of char-

acter who stereotypes his courtesy
into a list of memorized rules, who
keeps account of his good deeds and
bad deeds by number and charts them
at night, who figures his hopes of
heaven by the balance of credit on the
celestial ledger, and who so punctil-
iously goes his round of the commandments that his friends would
offer a hecatomb if only the man
would do a single impulsive and hearty
deed, were it even to be guilty of
spontaneous sin. Whichever way he
goes at it, negatively or positively,
this man is the legalist, living by rule
—the man of the one-mile spirit living
the one-mile life.

It was in escaping from this legalism
that Paul said he became a Christian.
No man is really a Christian until he
has escaped it. If a boy, adopted into
a strange home, and unruly in his new
surroundings, should perforce be given
a set of regulations which he must ob-
serve, he might become more orderly,
but he would hardly by that alone
become a true son. But if some day

the love of the father or mother should
be persuasively revealed to him, so
that the love that had been there always laid masterful hold on him, and
his love, newly born, should spring
up in answer, flooding his spirit with
its loyalty, and if, knowing the new
life in him, he should take the rules
and tear them up, saying "Because
I love you I will do all these and much
more beside," then a true son would
have been begotten. He would have
been "born again." "If ye love me, ye
WILL keep my commandments," said
Jesus and this statement of inevitable
consequence is summed up in Paul's
sublime word, "Love is the fulfilling
of the law." Apart from love a man
cannot keep so many rules or do so
many deeds as to make himself a
Christian. "If I give all my goods
to feed the poor and have not love,"
said Paul, "it profiteth me nothing!"
This does not mean the destruction of
the moral law; it means that the
Christian life so far outruns the moral
law, so far overflows commandment

34

Law the Molehill

with compassionate willingness to
serve, that rules of conduct are to its
wide domain what the obligations of
a civil marriage ceremony would be
to the love of Robert Browning and
Elizabeth Barrett. They would keep
the contract as one would walk over
a molehill in climbing a mountain!
Love does all that the commandments
say, and counts that the mere beginning. Love is not love until it has
forgotten rules. The Christian's
"royal law" fulfils all lesser laws like
the Atlantic flowing into the Bay of
Fundy when the sky calls to the tide.

Nor does this mean that conduct is
to be left to the unregulated expression of a compassionate heart. A man
may be in spirit truly courteous and
still need instruction in the conven-
tions of society. Love in the soul does
not make inevitable a judicious and
intelligent expression. So the old
proverb has it that " the chief business
of the wise is undoing the mistakes
made by the good." It is the prime
thing to be courteous and kindly at

heart, but important, too, to make the outer symbol truly signify the inner reality. "What is the use of being gold, if you look like brass?" is only partly true, but that part is of consequence. The love of God may be shed abroad in our hearts and still through ignorance that love's expression may be indiscreet and mischievous. While the primary matter, therefore, is that the branches abide in the vine, the trellis of commandment is a needful device that the fruit shall have guidance in normal growth. Nevertheless the trellis alone is so futile, and the training of a live vine so easy as compared with getting fruit from a dead one, that the necessity of the trellis should not blind us to the main issue which is the vital junction of the branch and vine. Moral instruction in details of conduct must never hide the fundamental matter, that there is no Christianity apart from a love which goes the second mile. Christ is witness that there is such a love, God himself underground in a man's life,

rising in artesian wells of living water
—a love so exhaustless in its willingness to serve, that he who knows it un-
derstands the safety of St. Augustine's
profound injunction, " Love God and
do as you please! "

This love that goes the second mile,
however, is more than a solvent for
moral drudgeries in the individual
life. It is distinctly a force of social
revolution. For here is the testing of
this principle in its application to society: that in the home it is entirely
possible to exercise this superabundant willingness to serve; in the neighborhood, even, it is possible for a man
to outrun the demands upon him by
the volunteering of his own kindliness; but who by any possibility can
live the spirit of the second mile in
the industrial world where the fundamental principle is

" The good old rule, the simple plan,
That he should get who has the
power,
And he should keep who can."

The Second Mile

Your business man will tell you frankly that it is hard enough to run an enterprise successfully and be scrupulously honest—honest, that is, not according to the letter of the statutes, but according to the dictates of a sensitive and instructed conscience. But when it comes to loving, loving in Jesus' sense of being twice as willing to help men as they are to ask you; as willing to give coat and cloak together as they can be to take your coat alone; willing to take two blows if two there must be, rather than give one; when it comes to overflowing all sense of duty with spontaneous kindliness, who does not see that the principles of Jesus and the principles of a competitive system where men throttle each other for bread come into absolute and unavoidable collision?

Even yet many Christians are incredulous that Christ ever intended that his principles should control the business world. The idea they work on is: Let love control in home, and school, in church and neighborhood, but let business be governed by the rules of battle. Yet is such a division of the world's life conceivably permanent? If the nation could not continue "half slave and half free," can the world continue so forever? Can a thoughtful man imagine as the ultimate state of society, the Kingdom of God on earth, a régime where home and neighborhood life shall be Christianized by the spirit of love and where the commercial world shall still be mastered by the spirit of " Every man for himself "? Surely it is manifest that Christ will not accept half a world for his demesne any more than he will accept half a man; and this is manifest, too, that before the spirit of the second mile, which now is possible in the home, shall come to its full possibility in the realm of business, our industrial system must be something other than it is to-day.

To be sure men can go the second mile always with certain individuals whom they know and like in business, but no one can make the spirit of the

second mile his commercial principle,
the underlying postulate of every
business transaction, when the basal
idea of the commercial system is ri-
valry for the necessities of life. To
be sure men can always ameliorate
the conditions of the competitive fight
so as to make its appearance more re-
spectable; they can always pass laws
to limit the degrees of exploitation
and abolish its worst indecencies.
Just so they smoothed out rough-and-
tumble fighting into the respectabili-
ties of the duel, guarded by regulations from brutality; but is duelling
any less abhorrent in principle than
thuggery? And is a system where one
man knifes another for food and clothes
any less abhorrent because restricting
laws tone down its more repugnant
features? No one doubts the benefi-
cent effect of making individual application of the spirit of kindliness in
business. But then, that is not the
primary idea of business in a competitive system. Mercy may be shown in
war, by one foe to another, and mu-

tual courtesy between individuals upon the firing line is an occurrence in almost every battle—only that is not what war means. And however many instances of kindliness between commercial rivals may relieve the fearful carnage of our industrial strife, the truth remains that men, instead of being in coöperative association to exploit the riches of the world, are rather engaged in exploiting one another; and that the basal idea of a war between men for life's necessities is violently at variance with Christ's idea of superabundant willingness to help. What first is needed is the Christian spirit of coöperation in the hearts of individuals, but with that must come the gradual reformation of social structure that such a spirit may have freedom of expression. This is what makes the great truth of Christ revolutionary if once it be really believed in. Let individuals do their best at it now, yet only in a commonwealth founded on coöperation can the second-mile spirit come to its full social utterance. And here is the question the twentieth-century Christian must settle—whether he really believes more in the principles of Christ, or the principles of the present industrial order. For unless irreconcilable enemies can live in the same house one or the other must go.

Returning now to the individual application of this master truth of Jesus there remains at least this one thing more to say: that not alone do the moral worth and joy of a man's life lie in the second mile, but the influence of a man lies there too. Jesus evidently is speaking here especially of some man who dislikes us, criticizes us, maliciously plans against us and seeks our hurt. What he says is that our love for that man should be so great that we should be more willing to serve him than he is to make us—yes, twice as willing; that no malice of his should ever reduce our souls to the level of hatred, or spoil our invincible love that pushes on through all his wrongs, still willing to serve him more and win him if we can.

There are many ways in which an unfriendly man can be treated, and every one has chances to try them all. "If he hurt me," it is possible to say, "I shall hurt him worse, until, like Jason sowing dragons' teeth and reaping a hostile army, he shall find his evil to me coming back upon him as many fold as I can manage it." That is vindictive vengeance. Or it may be said, "If he hurt me I shall, with level measure, return as much to him, and teach him the meaning of the law, 'Eye for eye, tooth for tooth.'" This is retribution. Or it may be said, "If he hurt me I shall ignore him, and scorning to recognize his injury, treat him with the contempt the moon gives to the dog that bays it." That is the disdain of hot resentfulness. Or it may be said, "If that man hurt me I will serve him still and try with undiscourageable love to do him good. Whatever comes, his hate shall never ruin my good will. I will take his unfriendliness as my opportunity for unrequited service, and when the first mile of his unkindness has been traveled I will be there to say, ' Man, my master is Christ and Christ never let any man's unkindness spoil His love. I am trying to follow Him and I am not going to let your unkindness spoil my love. You may not be my friend, but I am yours, and nothing you can ever do will stop it.' " That clearly is the way Jesus lived, and clearly that is what he expects of his disciples. To be sure, there may be limits which love cannot overpass; but then we may be certain that none of us has ever come within reaching distance of them. Even Christ seems never to have discovered limits to love in all his wide horizons.

Now this unconquerable compassion is not alone the most profoundly joyful spirit in which to live. At the very least it is that. The niggardly soul who, when he must give a quart of kindliness measures it out by thim-

The Only Hope

blefuls to avoid the possibility of surplus and does that only to the inner circle of his friends, has all the work and none of the joy of love. But this spirit of unwearied goodwill, that with a divine carelessness seeks just and unjust, is the great lifting power of the world, the secret not alone of joy but of spiritual effectiveness.

From the standpoint of the giver it seems a severe requirement that he love and serve those who have no personal claim on him, as Livingstone served Africa, or Paton the New Hebrides, but from the standpoint of Africa and the New Hebrides, which have no right to claim such devotion, the only hope lies in those souls who, like Livingstone and Paton, love of their own free will away over and above all right of demand. From the standpoint of the giver it is no easy matter to love regardless of the recipient's moral worth, like Moses praying God for the apostate people holding bacchanalian rout about their golden calf, but from the standpoint of the

45

The Second Mile

people who are unworthy, their only hope lies in just such souls, baptized with the spirit of saviorhood, who understand that "they who are sick need a physician," and are willing to help especially the undeserving. And it is a peculiarly hard saying that a man should love regardless of the personal attitude of the recipient, whether it be recognition and gratitude or the lack of them; but from the standpoint of the man so far down in spiritual desolation that he does not even know enough to be grateful, there is no hope save in those souls who for the time will forego gratitude and will serve on through ingratitude, misunderstanding, persecution even, if thereby they may be saviors of their fellows. The men with lifting power have always been men who served regardless of the right of the recipient to demand it, regardless of his moral worth, regardless of his personal ingratitude—who served for only one reason, the love of saving. Since the time when the "Lamb was slain be-

46

fore the foundation of the world," and the principle of sacrifice was imbedded in the fabric of the universe, there has been only one force with grip and lift enough in it to hoist the spiritual life of man, and that is the power Jesus used when he suffered, "the righteous for the unrighteous that he might bring us to God."

Now, mystical and unpractical as these injunctions may seem, as a matter of fact no spiritual achievement ever yet was wrought without this unbought and unpaid for generosity of love. The hope of the world's salvation lies in this spirit that, forgiving seventy times seven, keeps at the main issue which Jesus suggested when he said, "If thy brother hear thee, thou hast won thy brother." Whether in the individual's treatment of his private foe, or in society's treatment of her public enemy, the criminal, any other principle than this is not only wrong, it is entirely ineffective. This mercy may sometimes be stern; it may even take the outward form of punishment on the offender. So Beecher said, "A mother may have all Mount Calvary in her heart and all Mount Sinai in her hand: and the child get both." But whatever may be the outward form that wisdom determines to be best, the inner spirit is always of one quality, the undiscourageable desire to save.

This virtue of overflowing love that seeks alone the good of all men, is not too unpractical; it is too practical for this world of ours to understand. This kind of love is the only force that really gets things done. Without it not even an eddy has ever been made in the spiritual history of man. The men who have struck humanity's life as the shaft of water strikes the turbine at Niagara, saying, "Move," have been men who knew that "God does not always pay wages on a Saturday," and so were willing to serve on through all hostility, to help the very humanity that cursed them while they blessed. The roll-call of the world's spiritual heroes re-

All of Saviorhood

veals not a single one-mile man. For no man ever saved anybody, or served any great cause, or left any enduring impress who was not willing to forget indignities, bear no grudges, and, like Paul when the Jews had cast him out of their synagogues, had beaten, stoned, and all but killed him, say, " I could wish myself accursed for my brethren's sake, my kinsmen according to the flesh. . . . My heart's desire and prayer to God for Israel is that they may be saved." The world's saviors have all, in one way or another, loved their enemies and done them good. All of saviorhood lies in the second mile.

Clearly it is nothing less than this that Christianity means by love. The man who in his serving holds perpetual inquisition, suspicious that somehow he is being swindled out of love, and who, with the scrutiny of a detective, searches the character of his fellows for some unworthiness to excuse his neglect, never really loves at all, as Christianity counts it, whose

God "commended his love toward us in that while we were yet sinners Christ died for us." The man who serves for pay, and like a hireling loves with his eyes on Saturday noon, wondering if he will get his love's worth back again in the appreciation of his fellows, does not love at all, as Christ understood it who said, "Love your enemies, bless them that curse you, pray for them that despitefully use you."

This is the note that Jesus struck when he told his disciples that if they merely loved those who loved them or saluted their brethren only, they were doing what any outcast Publican would do. It is in the "exceeding righteousness" alone that mankind feels the touch of God. It is the spirit of the second mile that makes them seek the cause in the superhuman. To-day in a certain Chinese village, a strange deity receives incense at the pagan shrine. Long ago there came a Christian missionary there, who, before he could make

There God Is

clear the Christian doctrine, died. But it was not before he could make clear the spirit of his Christian love, that brought him unasked and unrewarded over seas to carry his good tidings and his ministry of help. And so they made him the village god and burn incense still upon his altar; for human nature is sure of this, that vicarious love is nearest deity. It is the instinct of the heart of man that where sacrificial love is, there God is also. There is one spirit whose divinity no man can deny and that is the unwearied compassion which indefatigably keeps on loving when love goes unrewarded. Even a Roman centurion cries, "The Son of God!" when a soul can bear the contumely and the pain of crucifixion and still pray, "Father forgive them." There is but one invincible power on earth and that is the unwearied spirit of the second mile.

Only, a man must surely believe in God to have it—in the God of Jesus and of immortality. For underneath such sacrificial compassion must lie the eternal love of God; and ahead of it must rise a vision radiant, a triumphal day, whose songs are even now in hours of struggle quietly audible,

" As if some fair city were one voice
    Around a king returning from his
        wars."

Here ends the Reading of this Book
Now for the Living of It